Muskaan**Y**uvraj

Motivation

LIFE LESSONS FROM BIKE-DRIVING
PART-1

Preface

I have been an avid bike rider for close to 35 years now (starting with the st bi-cycle I got after passing my 8th grade in school). It has been such an enlightening experience & over last 15 years I have realized that this passion has been giving subtle life lessons for me to have a little more discipline, a little more control over my life,

Sharing the same with you, hope these give you new perspectives of life, Happy Driving 😊

INDEX:

Chapter – 1: Conserve and pace your energy

While climbing uphill driving, it needs either hard paddling if its a bicycle or burn more fuel if its a bike, it would be not possible or rather very difficult if your legs are weak or you have limited fuel in the tank.

Above observation taught me that while dealing with a difficult situation in personal life or handling a complex professional assignment, one needs to ensure he has enough strength of resources be it enough manpower / budget / stakeholder buy-in well in advance (just like power in your legs to paddle or enough fuel to take your vehicle on the steep climb) since the uphill-tasks keep coming to you at un-expected intervals so always keep a tab on your resources (your money, relationships, health, equations with various stakeholders).

Chapter – 2: Handling big obstacles

While driving fast on a narrow road if the vehicle ahead is bigger in size, getting too close to this vehicle, vision for the traffic coming from the opposite direction gets very limited & can result in accident if you try overtaking all of a sudden but if a good distance is maintained from this bigger & slower vehicle ahead, you can overtake pretty safely & comfortably.

Above teaches that we need to widen our vision & should not get blinded by the size of the obstacle ahead of us by thinking too much (just like getting too close to bigger vehicle ahead on road) instead one should take a controlled decision by taking a pause mentally & time your overtaking from the obstacle on your path smoothly.

Chapter – 3: Remember the basics

You will always find another vehicle ahead of you while driving, either it moves away on its own or you overtake it if possible & when you succeed overtaking that vehicle ahead of you, you will find another vehicle ahead of you (I never find the road fully empty till my destination)

This teaches that life throws challenges/obstacles at every step of our journey & there will always be a next challenge awaiting, what matters is how you maintain your composure/discipline/basics/mental sanity overcoming each of those challenges enroute & still manage to enjoy the journey called life.

Chapter – 4: Don't be complacent or lose control

When climbing downhill if the vehicle is in neutral gear, its considered a risky driving pattern (as there are high chances of an accident in this scenario) & hence most of the time we engage the bike in a higher gear so that its a controlled / safe downhill passage.

Above teaches that when we are in a happy space & things are generally going as planned, precisely during this period we ought to be responsible in our behavior & not get carried away or else there will soon follow a downward spiral (like a vehicle coming downhill in a neutral gear)

Chapter – 5: You are in-charge of your life

Driving on a slope upwards requires me to put the bike in lower gear with increased throttle and correct use of the clutch to ensure the vehicle does not switch-off during the drive and while driving downhill its naturally quit comfortable.

It teaches me to be aware & plan the available resources (time/money/skills) appropriately as the situation demands.

Chapter-6: Don't forget to enjoy the journey

While speeding is a thrill to many however in the quest to reach faster, we not only put ourselves at higher risk but also miss the wonderful scenes that nature keeps throwing at the sideways of our path.

Life also is not a race but a journey to be enjoyed thoroughly, while we may be accelerating hard to climb up the ladder, we tend to overlook the joyful factors which often come in small packages like taking time off for a meaningful dialogue with your partner / spouse, sharing a hearty laugh with your parents, playing with kids or catching up with friends.

Chapter – 7: Make Friends, network on the way

During a long drive through highways / cities, we may have to halt or take breaks and during these if we connect with locals, they generally are helpful & more so in case of any emergency situations like vehicle failure, they will atleast guide to nearby correct place from where we can get help

Similarly during the journey called life, do not hesitate to connect with people on personal / professional level so that you can turn to them in case of any urgent situations as you never know when you will find yourself in trying circumstances and you may need help / necessary support from these same connections.

Chapter – 8: Preventive maintenance is key to longevity

f you treat your vehicle the same way as one of a family member, what I mean here is taking care about regular checks for any kind of niggling ssues it may have related to engine / oil / breaks / clutch plates / tyres etc, t will also pay you back through a solid driving experience without sudden breakdowns

Our physical / mental health also works the same way, treat your body and mind with care / regular checks on what you are feeding the body or mind with,

This will ensure a long / healthy / happy and most importantly a satisfied life.

Chapter – 9: Quality is very important

Peripheral parts of the vehicle like headlights / signal indicators / horn and very importantly tyres are generally ignored however these should be in top condition should you venture out on an adventurous trip or off-roading or on a long highway drive, it will ensure minimum risk to your journey till you reach your destination

We tend to ignore lot of areas in our life in our fascination to reach the destination like relationships / health / time / finances which can in turn jeopardize our goals / plans, we need to have a considerate / concerning approach to all these aspects to achieve goals in a full-filling and happy state to cherish the moment.

Chapter – 10: Know when to slow down or apply brakes

We get carried away in the need for speed and forget that on the road there can be speed breakers or pot holes or even sudden entry of people/stray animals crossing the road hence its absolutely essential that we are aware about the brakes & how soon can the vehicle stop before resuming further (**sometimes we use the speed as brakes by slowing the throttle of the accelerator without applying brakes, experienced drivers know about this and it can save fuel as well wear and tear** ☺)

Similarly learn to be aware of your surroundings in life and during the course of any important objectives that you are pursuing, take a pause every now and then to slow down, asses and channelize your efforts / energy whether they are in correct direction or on collision course, learn to use self-inertia to appropriately time your arrival to destination because correct timing is very important

Chapter – 11: Overload may result in sudden breakdown

Every vehicle has its kerb weight as well load capacity mentioned in the specifications, we may choose to take the additional load but that will have consequences like decreased fuel efficiency or increased maintenance cost

In the same way, understand your strengths, limits and take on the tasks which you can complete comfortably in time without affecting your physical health or draining yourself mentally or emotionally, do not over do or over commit yourself otherwise you may loose precious time recovering from the side effects.

Chapter – 12: Be practical rather than materialistic

Vehicle manufacturers provide standard gadgets / accessories which are confirming to design and are no way harmful yet so many people try experimenting with these aspects for example changing the exhaust / or may be engine cylinder bore for more power or pick-up and jazzy graphics just because someone else has done it (though its ok once in a while within limits)

We should also treat our life with the respect it deserves without bothering about what someone else is doing in his/her own life, what kind of clothes/accessories they are wearing or which destination they are going for vacationing because running after someone else's materialistic lifestyle will lead your own life very un-settled and frustrated.

Chapter – 13: Be responsive rather than reactive to situations

While cruising on a highway we may encounter a person who may be waiting to get a lift and also may be a house by the road on fire with people trying to douse that,

For the first instance, you may take a judgement looking at the body language of the person seeking lift and act accordingly,

While for the 2nd instance you may just take a short stop just check or to call the fire engine as it will not make much of difference if we get engaged for long dousing a house on fire since already lot of people are involved doing the same,

In life also there will be distractions or situations coming our way, they will warrant attention & our decision should be purely dependent on the type of situation,

We definitely should not run away if we can be someone's savior however in the same way we should not play an un-invited mediator should we encounter a potentially dangerous situation

we may choose to take a necessary action / step going by the gut feeling which may help getting the situation in control

Chapter – 14: Patience is the key

We face traffic jams or blockages more than ever nowadays, many of the people tend to get restless and start honking as if the traffic jam will be cleared by these actions, it will just add to the irritation and also other's on the road. Rather look for an open corner to steer your vehicle out of the jam or may be take a different route

We need to learn to be calm even under trying circumstances and face the challenges or delays in our life gracefully and with patience and acceptance of the situation, this way you will be able to make more appropriate decisions keeping your mental sanity in check.

Chapter – 15: Prepare, practice, repeat

A driving instructor will always try to make you follow basic rules pattern again and again because he knows that once out on the roads, this disciplined practicing of basics is going to make you a safe and responsible driver.

Apply the same logic in life, if you wish to have a sound and successful life, try to correct the basics like

- Having a constant morning routine,
- Habits,
- Diet,
- Communication skills

Practice deliberately irrespective of how mundane it may seem, learn to love the process and you will reach your goal or destination in life smoothly.

Chapter – 16: Problems do happen, learn to take them in your stride

Despite of how accurately we drive, there can be instances when we can meet with an accident however that doesn't stop us from driving

In the same way life will have un-expected scenarios popping up every now and then, do not lose motivation for your goals due to negative situations, take a pause, pray and thank the almighty universe and move on with your actions / efforts.

Chapter – 17: Plan your route before you get going

Nowadays google maps is much of a necessity specially on long drives it delivers for sure by alerting you of the distance / time and traffic situations

Just borrow the same logic and apply for any targeted goals or objectives through planning, estimation & budgeting, this will ensure greatly minimiz chances of failures or hiccups

Chapter – 18: Insurance is very important

Government and Traffic police gives importance to vehicle insurance not without a reason as it can prove to be lifesaving or life damaging

In the same way treat your body as a vehicle on which your as well as your family's aspirations are riding, a proper self-insurance (life/health/term) will provide the necessary cushion in case of eventualities

Chapter – 19: Wrong lane can be fatal

If we drive into wrong lane on a road or highway, no prizes for guessing what may happen & we will be totally on mercy of the oncoming vehicles from opposite directions

Similarly there is no substitute to the hard work or required efforts if you wish to achieve life or career goals, it may prove to be vastly detrimental should you choose to flirt with any short cuts, its your life, do not leave it to mercy of un-knowns.

Chapter – 20: Keep a tab on signboards

While driving in thoughts or mesmerized at the speedometer reading, we tend to forget to keep looking at the signboards or direction indicators resulting un-wanted delays and end up tired / irritated at the destination

Similarly life provides us vital clues / hints throughout our journey, some in the form of indicators that our body gives us which mean it wants us to slow down and not end up achieving our goals having a battered health which will snatch the joy of achievement. We also tend to overlook the finer signs of stress in our relationships or ignore friends in our zest for career goals & end up reaching the goals all alone, trust me there is no meaning of success if its achieved at the expense of without your near and dear ones

9 798735 150664